THE OFFICIAL

Freebies ®

for

Teachers

SOMETHING FOR NOTHING OR NEXT TO NOTHING!

By the Editors of *Freebies* Magazine

Illustrated by Catherine Leary

Lowell 🏠 House
Juvenile
Los Angeles

CONTEMPORARY BOOKS
Chicago

Lowell House books can be purchased at special discounts when ordered in bulk
for premiums and special sales. Contact Department JH at the following address:

Lowell House Juvenile
2029 Century Park East, Suite 3290
Los Angeles, CA 90067

Text Design: Cheryl Carrington

ISBN: 1-56565-373-4

Library of Congress Catalog Card Number is available.

Manufactured in the United States of America

10 9 8 7 6 5 4 3 2

Why Freebies?

"Why do they give it away?" Marketers, from companies large and small, are looking to win the battle for your dollars, and product sampling is an effective way to attract attention and make a positive impression. Studies show that allowing you to sample a company's product is more likely to result in a purchase than other marketing campaigns.

About This Book

Freebies for Teachers contains some great freebie offers that are sure to appeal to teachers and students alike, but you don't have to be a teacher to order from this book. Each offer has been described as accurately as possible to help you decide which offers are best for you.

Unlike offers in other "get things free" books, we have confirmed that each supplier wants you to have the offers listed in this book, and each supplier has agreed to have adequate stock on hand to honor all properly made requests. Many suppliers will make quantity discounts available. If you see something you like, write and ask about quantity discounts.

Some teachers have written and told us that they use the offers to set up a writing lesson in which students look through *Freebies for Teachers* and select an offer. The letter writing encourages good penmanship and spelling and the proper way to write a business letter.

How to Use Freebies for Teachers

1. **Follow the directions.** Each offer specifies how to order the freebie. Some offers may ask for an SASE (a long envelope that has your name and complete mailing address and a first-class postage stamp attached to it). Be sure to check the amount of postage requested. Some offers may require two first-class stamps. Likewise, offers from Canada will require the correct postage amount. Since postal rates

change, check with your local post office to determine the correct first-class postage to Canada. If a small postage and handling fee is requested (P&H), include the proper amount (a check or money order is usually preferred). Some suppliers may wait for out-of-town checks to clear before honoring requests. If you are sending coins, use a single piece of tape to tape them down.

2. **Print all information.** Not everyone's handwriting is easy to read. Neatly print your name, address, and the complete spelling of your city and state on your request. Be sure to include your return address on the outside of your mailing envelope. Use a ballpoint pen when you write, because pencils, felt tip pens, and ink pens smudge easily.

3. **Allow time for your request to be processed and sent.** Some suppliers send their offers by first-class mail. Others use bulk-rate mail, which can take up to eight weeks. Suppliers get thousands of requests each year and may process them slowly or right away, depending on the time of the year.

4. **What to do if you are unhappy with your freebie product.** If you are unhappy or have complaints about an offer, or if you have not received an offer within 8 to 10 weeks of your request, let *FREEBIES* know. Although the *FREEBIES* editors do not stock items or offer refunds from their offices, they can follow up on your complaints with any supplier. Suppliers that generate complaints will not be included in future editions. Send your complaints, comments, or suggestions, to:

> FREEBIES Book Editors
> 1135 Eugenia Place
> P.O. Box 5025
> Carpinteria, CA 93014-5025

5. **And there is more!** If you like the freebie offers in this book and want to see more free offers, then you should subscribe to *FREEBIES* Magazine. Five times a year, *FREEBIES* sends you a great magazine with approximately 100 current freebie

offers in each issue. Purchasers of *Freebies for Teachers* can get a special price on a one-year/five-issue subscription of only $4.95. (The regular subscription rate is $8.95—you'll save $4.00. See the special offer on page 79.)

Acknowledgments

It is difficult to put together a book of this nature without the help of talented and dedicated people working together. The staff at *FREEBIES* has a special thanks for the commitment of RGA/Lowell House to this project. Their support made it happen. Special mention must be given to Brenda Pope-Ostrow, Jessica Oifer, Cheryl Carrington, Rena Copperman, and the rest of the crew at RGA/Lowell House for the editing, the design, and the final push to complete this project.

Thank-yous are also reserved for Linda Cook, Jeff Girod, and Abel Magaña for their help and guidance, and thanks also to Courtney West. A special thanks to Stephanie O'Donnell for the research and coordination of the material in this book.

Drats! Coiled Again!

Cord Shortener

Keep cords safely and neatly tucked away with **5 Coilzit Cord Shorteners.** These 5" long, plastic cord shorteners are great for lamps, radios, televisions, clocks, venetian blinds, and draperies. Just wrap the cord around the Coilzit, tuck in the groove on the side, and your cord is neatly tucked away. The Coilzit Cord Shorteners help prevent accidents, short circuits, even electrical fires. The Coilzit is especially important to have in the presence of children.

Send: $2.00 P&H

Ask For: 5 Coilzit Cord Shorteners

Mail To: F & H Products
157 Greenbriar Drive
Chagrin Falls, OH 44022

Playing It Safe

Hidden Wallet

We lock the doors in our houses and schools because we want to keep our money and other valuables safe. When you're traveling or out shopping and need to take money with you, you should take similar precautions. You can keep your money safer by using the **hidden wallet.** This sturdy but lightweight, waterproof vinyl wallet hangs around your neck and stays hidden under your jacket or sweater. It has two zippered pockets big enough for money, credit cards, keys, and so on.

Send: $1.75 P&H

Ask For: Hidden Wallet

Mail To: Neetstuf, FR-90
P.O. Box 353
Rio Grande, NJ 08242

Getting Creative with Dates
. . . .
Date Recipes

California dates are nature's delicious, portable snack for today's life-on-the-go. Dates are high in fiber, a source of potassium, and free of sodium, fat, and cholesterol. Good nutrition never tasted so great! The **California Date Administration** is offering **FREE recipes** to assist you in cooking creatively with dates. The recipes range from desserts to dinners. With a little imagination, this simple fruit can add a delicious twist to an endless variety of recipes. Call for your FREE recipes now and start cooking!

Phone
Toll-Free: 1-800-223-8748

Winning the Germ War
. . . .
Safety Tips

Official estimates of annual cases of food-borne illness in the U.S. range from 6.5 to 33 million per year. The kitchen is the number one germ-infested area, harboring disease-causing bacteria you can't see or smell. With this in mind, a **FREE**, user-friendly **Kitchen Guide for Safe Food Preparation** has been developed by the Dial Corporation. The guide outlines specific ways to reduce the threat of bacteria and germs that cause food poisoning and other illnesses.

Phone
Toll-Free: 1-800-457-8739

Bringing You Reading with a Passion
....
Romantic Novel Magazine

Are you constantly looking for a novel to sweep you away from your everyday life? Well, look no further. *Romance Times Magazine*, published monthly, is the bible for the romance novel industry. The magazine includes reviews of each month's 150 new romance novels, details the comings and goings of celebrities, and interviews the most popular authors. Send for your sample issue to learn all about the hottest new romance novels.

Send: $2.00 P&H

Ask For: Sample Copy of *Romance Times Magazine*

Mail To: Romance Times Magazine
55 Berger St.
Brooklyn, NY 11211

Do the Can-Can at Home!
....
Canner's Catalog

For flavor, nutrition, and personal reward, nothing equals the rich tradition of home cooking, and the marketer of Ball Home Canning Products, Alltrista, has understood that for years. Send for your **FREE** copy of **Alltrista's Home Canners Catalog**, a collection of products for all who want to create long-lived memories in the kitchen. The company stands behind everything it offers, guaranteeing your satisfaction.

Send: Your name & address

Ask For: Home Canners Catalog

Mail To: Alltrista Corp.
Dept. FB
P.O. Box 2005
Muncie, IN 47307-0005

The Catfish Are Jumping!

Catfish Brochure

The catfish are jumping—genuine U.S. farm-raised catfish, that is—in **The Catfish Institute's FREE brochure**, which takes a look at the farm-raised catfish industry. The full-color brochure gives readers the inside story on catfish farming and the production process and explains how this traditional Southern delicacy is now the number-one farmed finfish and the fifth most popular fish in America. In addition, simple, tantalizing **catfish recipes** are featured, as well as consumer tips for selecting the freshest and safest seafood. Send for your FREE copy today.

Send: Your name & address
Ask For: Free Brochure
Mail To: Catfish: The Cultured Fish
P.O. Box 562
Gibbstown, NJ 08027

Ready, Set, Retire!

Book Offer

Confusion and apprehension are often the biggest obstacles to a secure retirement, says J. William Brimacombe, author of the **FREE book, *Ready, Set, Retire!*** The book is now being offered by John Hancock Financial Services as part of an effort to educate consumers and help them plan for their retirement. You'll discover that you can succeed against the increasing challenge of decreasing government and employer funding. In addition, you'll learn tax-smart strategies that can stretch your limited resources.

Phone Toll-Free: 1-800-828-7081, ext. 221
Note: Offer not valid in Maryland

Affordable Rewards

Silver Bracelet

Today, teachers have to make their lessons more and more interesting just to keep their students' attention. Now you can plan a classroom contest without spending big bucks on a first-place prize. Whether your winner is a boy or girl this **large, oval linked silver-plated bracelet** is the perfect prize. The bracelet measures 8" in length and is easily secured to the wrist with a bar and ring clasp. At this price, you may even want to order one for yourself!

Send: $2.00 P&H

Ask For: Silver-plated bar and ring clasp bracelet

Mail To: Jolene Brown
P.O. Box 842
Beatty, NV 89003

365 Days to Take Great Pictures

Camera Brochure

The Photography Information Council, dedicated to enhancing the joy of photography, has just published an easy-to-read, how-to **FREE brochure called "365 Days to Take Great Pictures,"** which covers basic photo tips and techniques. The photographs in this full-color, 16-page brochure were taken by today's leading photographers, and the text was written by experts in the photography industry. Topics include: School Days, Vacation Days, Indoor Days, Snow Days, Zoo Days, Earth Days, and Game Days. You'll also find tips on using and choosing cameras, filters, film, and accessories.

Phone
Toll-Free: 1-800-599-5929

Pediatric Mental Health
....
Health Newsletter

Teachers, find out how to protect your students' mental health, improve your relationships with special ed children, and deal with parents effectively. Send for a **FREE sample of Pediatric Mental Health**, an eight-page **newsletter** developed for Pediatric Projects Inc., a nonprofit organization. Each issue has summaries of research, interviews with educators, sources for specialized toys and books, and practical ideas to use in classrooms, counseling, and parent meetings.

Send: A long SASE with 2 first-class stamps

Ask For: Sample issue of Pediatric Mental Health newsletter

Mail To: Pediatric Mental Health
Pediatric Projects Inc.
P.O. Box 571-555
Tarzana, CA 91357

Shine at School
....
Shoe Shine Instructions

Kiwi Brands, the maker of convenient and innovative shoe care products, is helping teachers educate kids about the importance of self-image with a **FREE instruction sheet** for elementary classes K-4. **"Put Your Best Foot Forward—Steps to Proper Grooming Practices"** teaches children proper grooming and explains how they are keys in building successful futures. A Teacher's Guide is included as well as other money-saving offers and shoe care tips.

Send: A long SASE

Ask For: "Put Your Best Foot Forward" Lesson

Mail To: Kiwi Brands, Inc.
447 Old Swede Rd.
Douglassville, PA 19518-1239

School-Day Fun
School Fun Pack

Chase away school-day blues with this **school fun pack**. The set includes a wide assortment of 10 novelty mini erasers, 2 plastic stencils, plus 2 sheets each containing 12 iridescent stickers. Specify if it's for a girl or boy, and the supplier will send you a package with appropriate designs.

Send: $2.00 P&H

Ask For: School Fun Pack; specify boy or girl

Mail To: Surprises & Jewelry
P.O. Box 1052
Orange, CT 06477

A Program That Figures the Cost of Higher Education
College Financial Advice

When today's kindergarteners are ready to enter college, the average cost of a four-year stay at a public college is projected at $67,200 and $147,600 at private colleges. Knowing what a particular school will cost is the first step to developing a plan to pay for it. Introduced by John Hancock Financial Services, this **FREE computer diskette, "College Savings Plus,"** can instantly provide useful college information at the touch of a button. The disk comes in both IBM and Macintosh formats. Along with the disk, you will receive a comprehensive planning portfolio that includes brochures and workbooks to help prepare a child for college success.

Phone
Toll-Free: 1-800-633-1809, ext. 108

Expecting Good Advice

Health Brochure

Pregnancy is one of the most nutritionally demanding times of a woman's life. To help expectant moms deal with crucial health questions, The International Food Information Council has distilled the latest health information into these **2 FREE brochures: "Healthy Eating During Pregnancy"** reviews nutritional requirements of pregnant women, including the recommended weight gain, protein needs, vitamin and mineral supplementation, and the overall safety of foods in the diet; **"Caffeine and Women's Health"** sorts through the often conflicting reports on the health effects of coffee consumption and reviews the latest research on caffeine and women's health.

Send: A long SASE for each brochure requested

Ask For: "Healthy Eating During Pregnancy" and/or "Caffeine and Women's Health"

Mail To: IFIC Foundation
P.O. Box 1144, Dept. F1
Rockville, MD 20850

Boost Your Budget

Financial Newsletter

The *Budget Booster* is offering a **FREE** copy of their **newsletter** for people who want to minimize wasteful spending and get more out of their money. It's loaded with helpful tips, as well as money-saving recipes and craft ideas.

Send: A long SASE

Ask For: Sample copy of *The Budget Booster*

Mail To: Budget Booster
P.O. Box 992
Berwick, ME 03901

It's a Quiet Diet
· ·
Beano Tablets

Now you can make healthy food choices at lunchtime and maintain all the benefits of fiber without the uncomfortable side effects. Beano, a dietary supplement, contains a natural food enzyme that improves the digestibility of "gassy" foods such as broccoli, cabbage, beans, and whole grain cereals and bread. Send for a **FREE sample of Beano tablets,** and you will also receive money-saving coupons good toward your next store purchase.

**Phone
Toll-Free:**   1-800-257-8650
Ask For: Beano Tablets Sample

Contractor Tips
· · · · · · · · · · · · · · · · · · · ·
Financial Guide

If you're planning to make major improvements that require the services of a licensed contractor, you need this **brochure.** The **FREE "Survival Guide to Avoiding Contractor Rip-Off"** offers a foundation of information and solid advice on what to do when using a contractor. For your benefit, the advice presented in this guide was prepared by a licensed contractor.

Send: A long SASE
Ask For: "Contractor's Survival Guide"
Mail to: Multi-Trade Associates
3720 Corta Calle
Pasadena, CA 91107

Home, Safe Home
••••••••••••••••••
Safety Packet

In response to the thousands of avoidable deaths and millions of disabling injuries that occur each year as a result of home safety-related incidents, Lowe's Home Safety Council has established a unique toll-free information line to help consumers protect themselves and their families. Call **1-800-4-SAFE HOME** to access prerecorded messages on a range of important home issues that affect children and adults. Topics include: child safety, fire safety, senior safety, security, and pet safety. The line is accessible 24 hours a day, 7 days a week. Consumers who call can also receive a **FREE home safety information packet**, which includes a comprehensive full-color magazine.

Phone
Toll-Free: 1-800-4-SAFE HOME

How Long Will Your Money Last?
••••••••••••••••••
Financial Guides

Many people want to retire as early as possible, but don't have enough money to do it and still live a comfortable lifestyle. Now you can find out just how much money you'll need when you retire with this **FREE reference card**, "How much time until the money runs out?" You'll also receive a **FREE copy of the latest issue of *Bill Staton's Money Advisory**, "America's most user-friendly financial newsletter." It's chock full of money-making and money-saving ideas.

Send: A long SASE with 2 first-class stamps
Ask For: "How Long Will My Money Last?"
Mail To: The Financial Training Group
300 East Bl., B-4
Charlotte, NC 28203

Science Project Plan

Project Ideas

Even Dr. Frankenstein occasionally got stuck while brainstorming ideas for his science projects. But *you* can get help with **1 FREE science project instruction sheet**, plus a listing of over 250 available plans and demonstrations. The FREE project instructions include a materials list and a helpful illustration of what each project should look like when completed.

Send: Your name & address and 2 loose first-class postage stamps

Ask For: A Science Project Instruction Sheet

Mail To: The Mad Scientist
P.O. Box 124
Elkmont, AL 35620

A Penny Earned

Money-Saving Tips

You're not cheap—you just want to be careful how you spend your earnings. You're just the kind of person who would appreciate a **FREE sample issue of *A Penny Saved.*** This timely newsletter is designed for middle-class people who are trying to save and spend their money wisely. The eight-page monthly publication addresses all aspects of financial well-being, including saving money on groceries, tax advice, inexpensive home decorating, and more.

Send: A long SASE

Ask For: Sample copy of *A Penny Saved*

Mail To: A Penny Saved
RR 5, Box 67
Council Bluffs, IA 51503

Safety for Kids
Safety Packet

Teachers and parents have a lot to be concerned about these days, and the safety of children is usually at the top of the list. This **FREE "My Safety Rules" bookmark and "Checklist for Parents"** help educate teachers, parents, and kids about potential dangers. The laminated bookmark, produced in conjunction with the National Center for Missing & Exploited Children, lists eight valuable tips for protecting children and two toll-free numbers for more advice.

Send: A long SASE

Ask For: "My Safety Rules" Bookmark & Parents' Checklist

Mail To: Twin Sisters Productions, Inc.
1340 Home Ave., Ste. D
Akron, OH 44310

"Cutting" School
School Financial Guide

Learn how to cut back on school expenses in this **FREE eight-page report, "Back to School Savings with the *Skinflint News*,"** which suggests ways you and your students can save on school supplies, clothes, lunches, and time. The publishers will also send you a **FREE copy of the *Skinflint News*,** their nationally circulated monthly newsletter of thrifty advice for all areas of your life.

Send: A long SASE

Ask For: Back to School Tips & Sample copy of *Skinflint News*

Mail To: Skinflint News—Back to School
P.O. Box 818
Palm Harbor, FL 34682

Best Western Where Guide

Travel Guide

The *1996 North American Best Western Road Atlas and Travelers' Guide* provides information and maps for more than 2,000 Best Western hotels in the United States, Canada, Mexico, the Caribbean, and Central America. Besides hotel information, this **FREE 292-page guide** lists many points of interest. Also included is an eight-panel fold-out pamphlet on "Traveler Safety Tips."

Phone
Toll-Free: 1-800-528-1234
Ask For: *1996 North American Best Western Road Atlas and Travelers' Guide*

Read 'Em & Sweep

Sweepstakes Information

Sweepstakes and contests offer exciting opportunities to win valuable prizes and money while playing in the comfort of your home. Literally thousands of prizes are given away every month by major companies. Learn how you can increase your odds of being in the money with a **FREE sample issue of** *Sweeping the USA*, a four-page newsletter that includes winning tips, ideas, and up-to-date sources of national sweepstakes.

Send: A long SASE
Ask For: Sample copy of *Sweeping the USA*
Mail To: Delosh
171 Water St.
Massena, NY 13662

The Way to Go
Car Rental Information

If you've ever been confused over the endless number of options available when choosing a rental car "**A Consumer's Guide to Renting a Car**," FREE from Alamo Rent A Car, can help. It's a handy glove-box-sized booklet that helps you be a smart consumer. It even includes a comparison worksheet that allows you to determine which rental company offers you the best deal.

Send: A long SASE with 2 first-class stamps

Ask For: "A Consumer's Guide to Renting a Car"

Mail To: Alamo Rent A Car
P.O. Box 13005
Atlanta, GA 30324

Water Wise
Gardening Tips

To help conserve water, DIG Corporation has created a **FREE booklet entitled "Wise Watering for Beautiful Gardens."** Filled with color photos and informative illustrations, the easy-reading booklet contains useful gardening suggestions for creating and maintaining a water-wise, efficient landscape. Also included are $4 worth of rebate coupons for DIG drip watering kits.

Send: A long SASE

Ask For: "Wise Watering for Beautiful Gardens" Brochure

Mail To: DIG Corp.
130 Bosstick Blvd.
San Marcos, CA 92069

Vanna Glass of Milk?
• • • • • • • • • • • • • • • • • • • •
Milk Brochure

Learn surprising facts about milk and why celebrities like Vanna White, Lauren Bacall, Christie Brinkley, and others are proudly sporting milk mustaches by calling **1-800-WHY-MILK.** Available 24 hours a day, 7 days a week, you can ask specific questions of dieticians and registered nurses, or browse through a series of recorded messages on topics such as milk's role in a healthy lifestyle and great low-fat milk recipes. You'll also receive a **FREE copy of a 12-page brochure, "Milk, What a Surprise!"**

Phone
Toll Free: 1-800-WHY-MILK

#1 Onion
• • • • • • • • • • • • • • • • • • •
Recipes

The Vidalia Onion, grown only in twenty counties in Southeast Georgia, is called the "world's sweetest onion." To help you experience its distinctive taste, the Vidalia Onion Committee offers this **FREE collection of recipes.** Salads, salsas, sandwiches, side dishes, and main dishes showcase the versatility and unique taste of Vidalias. And like the onion itself, which is fat free and low in calories, all the recipes are low in fat and loaded with luscious flavor.

Send: A long SASE
Ask For: "Vidalia Onions" Brochure
Mail To: Vidalia Onion Committee, Dept. F
P.O. Box 1609
Vidalia, GA 30474

Be Sure with BreathAsure

BreathAsure Capsules

BreathAsure is a unique breath freshener that works internally with your digestive system—the source of bad breath. This 100% natural product fights bad breath caused by garlic, onions, and other pungent foods. It even fights morning breath. Send for a **FREE single-use packet of BreathAsure.** This unique blend of parsley seed and sunflower oil in a soft capsule contains no artificial flavors, colors, preservatives, alcohol, or sugar.

Send:	A long SASE
Ask For:	Single-Use Pack of BreathAsure
Mail To:	BreathAsure, Dept. SUP
	26115 Mureau Rd.
	Calabasas, CA 91302-3126
Limit:	1 per address

Pack Your Bags

Travel Tips

Never pay full price for travel. A **FREE sample issue of** *The Thrifty Traveler* monthly newsletter will show you how to stretch your travel dollars, whether you're just traveling around the country or around the world. Each issue is jam-packed with news, tips, resources, and special deals. Normally $2.50, this FREE issue is available ONLY to FREEBIES readers. You'll also receive a special subscription offer.

Send:	A long SASE
Ask For:	Sample copy of *The Thrifty Traveler*
Mail To:	The Thrifty Traveler
	P.O. Box 8168-F
	Clearwater, FL 34618

Better with Buttermilk
· · · · · · · · · · · · · · · · · · · ·
Low-Fat Recipes

A touch of buttermilk can make anything you bake better. You'll find all the goodness of real churned buttermilk in Saco's Cultured Buttermilk Blend. Try a **FREE 1 oz. sample of Saco Buttermilk Blend,** the convenient, contemporary way to bring back that country-fresh, old-fashioned flavor. You'll also receive a set of **11 low-fat recipes,** helpful hints for a healthier diet, and money-saving coupons on other Saco products available at your local grocer.

Phone Toll-Free: 1-800-373-7226

Ask For: Low-Fat Recipes & Saco Buttermilk Sample

Limit: 1 per address

Sweep Success
· · · · · · · · · · · · · · · · · · · ·
Sweepstakes Newsletter

F ind out how you can enter hundreds of contests and sweepstakes by getting a **FREE sample issue of** *Best Sweepstakes Newsletter.* Thousands of lucky people win huge sums of cash and big prizes through corporate-sponsored sweepstakes. Every month this 12-page newsletter publishes details on interesting editorials and approximately 30 current contests. As a bonus, you'll also receive a **FREE sample issue of** *Best Extra,* a 4-page bulletin that features short-running sweepstakes.

Send: A long SASE with 2 first-class stamps

Ask For: Sample copy of *Best Sweepstakes Newsletter* & *Best Extra*

Mail To: BSN
4215 Winnetka Ave. N., Ste. 219
New Hope, MN 55428

In A Zone

Workout Tips

Would you like to become the best runner you can be? Whether you want to set a new personal record or reduce your risk of injuries, monitoring your heart rate can help you achieve your goals. How? Monitoring your heart on a consistent basis helps you detect—and therefore avoid—dehydration, lack of recovery from a workout, over-training, and possible injury. Send for a **FREE brochure entitled "Target Heart Rate Zone Running"** to get the details on developing a smart course.

Send: A long SASE

Ask For: "Target Heart Rate Zone Running" Brochure

Mail To: AR & FA
4405 E. West Hwy., Ste. 405
Bethesda, MD 20814

Nail Care By Mail

Nail Care Tools

Realys Incorporated has been the supplier for professional manicurists for over ten years. And now they want to put one of their best nail tools right in your hands. Send for your **FREE Realys washable nail file** from their new line of professional quality products for consumers.

Send: A long SASE

Ask For: Realys Washable Nail File

Mail To: Realys Professional Nail Care
7601 Woodwind Dr.
Huntington Beach, CA 92647

Quilty As Charged

Quilt Patterns

A well-made quilt is a priceless heirloom. Send for a **package of quilt patterns** and make your own hand-crafted treasures. Choose from these three separate projects: "Afternoon Tea," a set of table dressings; "Classic Cornice Quilts," curtains with two coordinating valances; and "Appliqued Floor Quilts," decorative floor throws. Each project includes a list of materials, full-sized patterns, and a color picture of the finished work.

Send: $2.00 P&H for each project

Ask For: Quilt Project; specify Tea, Cornice, and/or Floor

Mail To: Stitcher's Marketplace
P.O. Box 411
New Albany, OH 43054-0411

Doll-a-Rama

Doll Patterns

I f you are interested in making dolls, send for a **sample issue** of *Keeping You in Stitches*. This fun newsletter combines a conversational writing style with some adorable illustrations to bring you the smartest tips and latest ideas in doll making. The newsletter also includes patterns for making a cloth doll, a 4" felt teddy bear, and a sweater to fit 10" to 22" dolls (a $20 value!). Plus, you can order more patterns for an Elvis, a Marilyn Monroe, or an Angel Baby doll.

Send: $1.00 P&H

Ask For: Sample Issue of *Keeping You in Stitches*

Mail To: Joan Jansen
P.O. Box 85
Monterey Park, CA 91754

A Full Refund
Refund Magazine

Refund World is a monthly bulletin that combines the latest refund offers with important information about consumer products, including recall notices and new product releases. Send for a **FREE sample issue of *Refund World***, and you'll be on the pipeline to receive hundreds of refund offers from all over the country—many of which are only advertised locally but are valid nationally. Complete details are provided for obtaining each refund.

Send:	2 loose first-class postage stamps and your name & address (on an address label if possible)
Ask For:	Sample copy of *Refund World*
Mail To:	Refund World Box 16001 Philadelphia, PA 19114
Limit:	1 per address

Go Back in Time
Anti-Aging Cream

Want to look younger? Use this 5 oz., 15-day **sample of Retinol A** twice a day and see astounding results within a short time. Retinol A nourishes and protects your skin while combating the visual signs of aging. So what are you waiting for? Order today and turn back the hands of time.

Send:	$1.00 P&H
Ask For:	Retinol A Sample
Mail To:	21st Century Cosmetics Dept. RA124 10 Chestnut St. Spring Valley, NY 10977
Limit:	1 per address

Take Your Cuts

Refund Magazine

Learn from *Family Circle's* refund and coupon expert, Susan Samtur, with a copy of her national publication *Refundle Bundle.* This monthly 48-page refund and coupon guide contains more than 400 offers made by every conceivable manufacturer. *Refundle Bundle* also reports on consumer news such as recalls, product introductions, and details tips and ideas contributed by readers.

> **Send:** $1.00 P&H (postage stamps accepted)
>
> **Ask For:** Issue of *Refundle Bundle*
>
> **Mail To:** Select Coupon Club
> Box 338-FB
> Tuckahoe, NY 10707

A Free Taste

Recipes

Tired of trying to spice up the same old meals? Send for **Gloria Pitzer's FREE flyer with 15 sample Secret Recipes.** "The Recipe Detective," as she is commonly known, has been recreating the most popular secret recipes for the past 20 years. Some of her most requested are: Recess Peanut Butter Cups, Famous Nameless Chocolate Chip Cookies, Big Bucket in the Sky Fried Chicken, and Lone John Silver Fish and Chips.Your offer will also tell you how to order the *Secret Recipe* newsletter and cookbook.

> **Send:** A long SASE
>
> **Ask For:** 15 Sample Secret Recipes
>
> **Mail To:** Gloria Pitzer's Secret Recipes
> P.O. Box 237
> Marysville, MI 48040

Cleaning Made Easy
• • • • • • • • • • • • • • • • • •
All-Purpose Cleaner

Is there an easy way to clea[...]
for a **trial package of Protect A**[...]
contains samples of the "Quick & Easy W[...]
Wax & Treatment" formulas. "Quick & Easy[...]
you to wash an entire vehicle without a water hose[...]
Protect All "Polish, Wax & Treatment" cleans, polishe[...]
treats *all* surfaces—leaving an antistatic, water repellent, sh[...]
on hard surfaces, while protecting vinyl, rubber, and plastic.[...]
Great for vehicles, home, school, and office applications.

Send: $1.00 P&H

Ask For: Protect All "Duopak"

Mail To: Protect All, Inc.
P.O. Box 5968
Orange, CA 92613-5968

Horsing Around
• • • • • • • • • • • • • • • • • •
Sewing Patterns

Remember those make-believe horses you made out of broom handles when you were young? Get ready to saddle up again with this **set of stick horse patterns.** With a few easy-to-find supplies and these full-sized patterns, you and your students can make five different styles of horses, including unicorn, Christmas, Valentine, patriotic, and Western designs.

Send: $1.50 P&H

Ask For: Stick Horse Patterns

Mail To: Peebles Western Patterns
P.O. Box 234
Dupuyer, MT 59432

there is more than one answer to a problem. ...h is the case with these **compact "I.Q."** games. ...llenge is to find as many different arrangements of ...zzle pieces as possible. Choose from 2 different ...s: an I.Q. Block or an I.Q. Circle. The block can be ...bled in more than 60 different ways, while there are ... than 10 variations to solve the Circle. Each game is ... contained in a plastic case that measures about 3" across. *...tion:* Because of the small colorful pieces, these games are ...ly safe for ages six and up.

Send: $2.00 P&H

Ask For: I.Q. Game; specify Circle or Block

Mail To: Neetstuf, FR91
P.O. Box 908
Rio Grande, NJ 08242

Paper Jungle

Paper Garland

Hang the streamers from the ceiling because it's time to party! This **8' paper garland** is the perfect decoration for a classroom party or just for fun. The garland measures about 3" wide and features a detailed illustration of a group of cute baby wild animals. The design repeats every five inches.

Send: $1.00 P&H

Ask For: Paper Garland

Mail To: Kaye's Holiday, Dept. MA
6N021 Meredith Rd.
Maple Park, IL 60151

Really Good Bread

Bread Samples

In 1977 a gentleman named Sam opened a bakery to produce and sell his favorite bread, baked from a family recipe that dates back to the early 1900s. Opening up that bakery turned out to be a great idea for "Father Sam" and the public, both reaped the benefits of that great bread. Sam soon decided to share this delightful bread with as many people as possible. Now you can try a **14-oz. package of Father Sam's Medium White Pocket Bread.** The FREEBIES staff loved it, and you're sure to like it, too!

Send: $2.00 P&H

Ask For: Sample of Father Sam's Pocket Bread

Mail To: Father Sam's Pocket Bread
P.O. Box 848
N. Tonawanda, NY 14120-0848

Academic Awards

Award Ribbons

No teacher should be without a ready supply of premiums to reward students. This assortment of award ribbons provides the right kind of positive reinforcement. Send for a **set of 2 award ribbons** from these choices: Student of the Month, Perfect Attendance, Music, Reading, Science, Spelling, Honor Roll, and Birthday. Each ribbon is 2" x 8" and crimp cut at the top and bottom.

Send: $1.00 P&H

Ask For: Classroom Ribbons; specify choices

Mail To: Fax Marketing
460A Carrollton Dr.
Frederick, MD 21701

Freedom of Speech
••••••••••••••••••••••
Speech Therapy Brochure

Teachers often report difficulty in knowing how to deal with a child who stutters. Stuttering is one of the most misunderstood disabilities. To provide counseling for educators, the Speech Foundation of America offers a **FREE brochure entitled "The Child Who Stutters at School: Notes to the Teacher."** This six-panel pamphlet gives practical tips for various situations that will maximize the child's learning experience and minimize the stress.

Send: Your name & address

Ask For: "The Child Who Stutters at School: Notes to the Teacher"

Mail To: Stuttering Foundation of America
P.O. Box 111749
Memphis, TN 38111-0749

College Scholarships
••••••••••••••••••••••
College Financial Advice

Everyone knows of the high cost of college tuition. Here is a chance to receive a **sample issue of *The College Planner Newsletter,*** which will help you locate scholarships for your students or your own kids. This eight-page publication outlines scholarships available from private companies, corporations, foundations, and organizations. Also included are tips on saving money during college and postgraduate strategies for landing a job.

Send: $1.00 P&H

Ask For: Sample of *The College Planner Newsletter*

Mail To: The College Planner, Inc.
P.O. Box 940793
Maitland, FL 32794-0793

Special Ed

*Special Education
Newsletter*

Teachers of "Special Education" students may want to send for a **FREE sample issue of *SpEds Newsletter.*** Published monthly (September through May) by a group of educators with 35 years of experience in the field, the 8-page newsletter provides support to teachers and parents by allowing them to share ideas with other readers. Each issue contains interesting articles, effective strategies, and activities for the special education student.

Send: A long SASE with 2 first-class stamps
Ask For: Sample copy of *SpEds Newsletter*
Mail To: SpEds
1948 Sandee Crescent
Virginia Beach, VA 23454

The Skinny on Fat

Health Tips

The low fat vs. nonfat dilemma can be very confusing. Help get the facts straight with this **FREE brochure direct from the California Olive Industry**, which gives a quick education on how to make correct choices. It explains the different kinds of fat and shows you how to apply this knowledge to make proper food selections. A **FREE bookmark** is included to keep in your cookbook as a healthy, fat-friendly reminder!

Send: Your name & address
Ask For: "The Skinny on Fat"
Brochure/Bookmark Offer
Mail To: California Olive Industry
Dept. SFF
P.O. Box 7796
Fresno, CA 93747

Sensible Ideas for a Greener World

Environmental Newsletter

Somebody has to protect the world, and it might as well be you. So send away for a **FREE sample of *Practically Green***, the newsletter that will get you and your students motivated to help save the environment. This newsletter is geared to anyone who wants to help create a "greener" world but who needs an extra jump start. Each issue has useful and stimulating ideas on how to reuse products and recycle waste. Grab a stamp and send for this FREE sample issue offer.

Send: A long SASE

Ask For: Sample copy of *Practically Green*

Mail To: Practically Green
4326 SE Woodstock Bl. #500F
Portland, OR 97206

Confidence Encapsulated

BeSure Capsules

Attention, ladies and gentlemen. Now you can eat beans and vegetables with confidence. By requesting this **FREE offer from the makers of BeSure Capsules**, you'll be sure you won't experience embarrassing flatulence. A capsule before eating will eliminate intestinal gas before it starts. The product is allergy safe and effective with both hot and cold foods. Call the toll-free telephone number today!

**Phone
Toll-Free:** 1-800-688-3933

Audio Amigo
Language Cassette

Because most American students are not exposed to different languages at a young age, it is often difficult to determine which language to study in school. For this reason, award-winning Twin Sisters Productions has designed a **30-minute audiocassette** to help teachers and students become familiar with Spanish, French, German, and Italian. Using fun songs, rhythm, and teaching strategies, students learn basic words and phrases in each language.

Send: $3.00 P&H

Ask For: "Which Language Would You Like to Learn?" Audiocassette

Mail To: Twin Sisters Productions, Inc.
1340 Home Ave., Ste. D
Akron, OH 44310

It's in the Clouds
Weather Guide

A change in the weather seldom comes as a surprise to those who recognize nature's signals. If you are interested in a scientific approach to weather predicting, send for this **pocket guide on "How to Forecast the Weather."** This 10-page booklet will give you and your students information on foretelling the weather and presents full-color photos of various sky patterns. It also offers facts on wind and lightning.

Send: $1.00 P&H

Ask For: "How to Forecast the Weather" Booklet

Mail To: Cloud Chart Inc.
P.O. Box 21298
Charleston, SC 29413

Wonder Feet
Wonder Walkers

Live and work on your feet? Wonder Walkers high-performance insole liners provide the ultimate in shock protection, cushioning comfort, and durability. These insoles regularly sell for $5.95, but now you can try a **pair of Wonder Walkers** for just a small shipping fee. Wonder Walkers not only benefit your feet, but your legs, knees, and back, and they retain over 95% of their original cushioning even after hundreds of miles!

Send: $2.00 P&H

Ask For: Sample Pair of Wonder Walkers; specify women's or men's and shoe size

Mail To: Footsmart Products
Dept. 18
P.O. Box 181002
Memphis, TN 38181

Limit: 1 per address

Give Us a Sign
Sign-Language Postcards

Did you know that sign language is the third-most-used language in America? Open yourself and your students to a new world of communication—learn basic signing with a **set of 3 postcards** that each illustrate the entire manual alphabet. They're great for classroom decor and even for teaching young children the basic sign language alphabet.

Send: $1.00 P&H

Ask For: 3 Sign Language Postcards

Mail To: Keep Quiet
Box 367
Stanhope, NJ 07874

Fantastic Freebies

I'M A FAN!

Most professional sports franchises have free materials, such as season schedules and ticket information, that they give to enthusiastic fans. Some teams even give fan packages that may contain stickers, photos, fan club information, catalogs, and more.

To get these great items, all you need to do is write to your favorite team, include your name and address, then ask for a **"fan package."**

We've compiled the addresses of all the professional baseball, basketball, football, and hockey teams. Although not all teams require it, we recommend you send a long SASE to help speed up your request. Be sure to include proper postage for all teams based in Canada. The post office can tell you the current postal rates.

Here's another tip: If you want to contact a specific player on your favorite team, address the envelope to his attention. Keep in mind that because of the high volume of fan mail each team receives, it may take eight weeks or more for a response.

AMERICAN LEAGUE BASEBALL TEAMS

Baltimore Orioles
333 West Camden St.
Baltimore, MD 21201

California Angels
P.O. Box 2000
Anaheim, CA 92803

Boston Red Sox
4 Yawkey Way
Boston, MA 02115

Chicago White Sox
333 W. 35th St.
Chicago, IL 60616

Cleveland Indians
Jacobs Field
2401 Ontario Street
Cleveland, OH 44115

Detroit Tigers
Public Relations
Tiger Stadium
Detroit, MI 48216

Kansas City Royals
P.O. Box 419969
Kansas City, MO 64141

Milwaukee Brewers
201 S. 46th St.
Milwaukee, WI 53214

Minnesota Twins
501 Chicago Ave. South
Minneapolis, MN 55415

New York Yankees
Yankee Stadium
Bronx, NY 10451

Oakland Athletics
Oakland Coliseum
Oakland, CA 94621

Seattle Mariners
P.O. Box 4100
Seattle, WA 98104

Texas Rangers
The Ballpark in Arlington
P.O. Box 90111
Arlington, TX 76004

Toronto Blue Jays
SkyDome
One Blue Jay Way
Suite 3200
Toronto, Ontario,
Canada M5V 1J1
*(Note: first-class mail to
Canada requires extra stamps)*

NATIONAL LEAGUE BASEBALL TEAMS

Atlanta Braves
P.O. Box 4064
Atlanta, GA 30302

Chicago Cubs
Wrigley Field
1060 West Addison St.
Chicago, IL 60613

Cincinnati Reds
100 Riverfront Stadium
Cincinnati, OH 45202

Colorado Rockies
1700 Broadway
Suite 2100
Denver, CO 80290

Florida Marlins
2267 NW 199th St.
Miami, FL 33056

Houston Astros
P.O. Box 288
Houston, TX 77001

Los Angeles Dodgers
1000 Elysian Park Ave.
Los Angeles, CA 90012

Montreal Expos
P.O. Box 500
Station M
Montreal, Quebec,
Canada H1V 3P2
*(Note: first-class mail to
Canada requires extra stamps)*

New York Mets
Shea Stadium
Flushing, NY 11368

Philadelphia Phillies
P.O. Box 7575
Philadelphia, PA 19101

Pittsburgh Pirates
P.O. Box 7000
Pittsburgh, PA 15212

St. Louis Cardinals
250 Stadium Plaza
St. Louis, MO 63102

San Diego Padres
P.O. Box 2000
San Diego, CA 92112

San Francisco Giants
Candlestick Park
San Francisco, CA 94124

NATIONAL BASKETBALL ASSOCIATION TEAMS

Atlanta Hawks
One CNN Center
South Tower, Suite 405
Atlanta, GA 30303

Boston Celtics
151 Merrimac St.
5th Floor
Boston, MA 02114

Charlotte Hornets
One Hive Drive
Charlotte, NC 28217

Chicago Bulls
One Magnificent Mile
980 N. Michigan Ave.
Suite 1600
Chicago, IL 60611

Cleveland Cavaliers
2923 Streetsboro Rd.
Richfield, OH 44286

Dallas Mavericks
Reunion Arena
777 Sports St.
Dallas, TX 75207

Denver Nuggets
1635 Clay St.
Denver, CO 75207

Detroit Pistons
The Palace of Auburn Hills
Two Championship Dr.
Auburn Hills, MI 48326

Golden State Warriors
Oakland Coliseum Arena
Oakland, CA 94621

Houston Rockets
The Summit
10 Greenway Plaza
Houston, TX 77046

Indiana Pacers
300 East Market St.
Indianapolis, IN 46204

Los Angeles Clippers
L.A. Sports Arena
3939 S. Figueroa St.
Los Angeles, CA 90037

Los Angeles Lakers
Great Western Forum
3900 W. Manchester Blvd.
Inglewood, CA 90306

Miami Heat
Miami Arena
Miami, FL 33136

Milwaukee Bucks
Bradley Center
1001 N. Fourth St.
Milwaukee, WI 53203

Minnesota Timberwolves
Target Center
600 First Ave. North
Minneapolis, MN 55403

New Jersey Nets
Meadowlands Arena
East Rutherford, NJ 07073

New York Knickerbockers
Madison Square Garden
2 Penn Plaza, 3rd Floor
New York, NY 10121

Orlando Magic
Orlando Arena
One Magic Place
Orlando, FL 32801

Philadelphia 76ers
Veterans Stadium
Broad St. & Pattison Ave.
Philadelphia, PA 19148

Phoenix Suns
P.O. Box 1369
Phoenix, AZ 85001

Portland Trail Blazers
Suite 600 Lloyd Building
700 NE Multnomah St.
Portland, OR 97232

Sacramento Kings
One Sports Parkway
Sacramento, CA 95834

San Antonio Spurs
Alamodome
100 Montana St.
San Antonio, TX 78203

Seattle Supersonics
190 Queen Anne Ave. North
Suite 200
Seattle, WA 98109

Toronto Raptors
150 York St.
Suite 1100
Toronto, Ontario,
Canada M5H3S5
*(Note: first-class mail to
Canada requires extra stamps)*

Utah Jazz
Delta Center
301 West South Temple
Salt Lake City, UT 84101

Vancouver Grizzlies
NBA Vancouver
780 Beatty St., 3rd Fl.
Vancouver,
British Columbia,
Canada V6B2M1
*(Note: first-class mail to
Canada requires extra stamps)*

Washington Bullets
One Harry S. Truman Dr.
Landover, MD 20785

AMERICAN CONFERENCE FOOTBALL TEAMS

Buffalo Bills
One Bills Dr.
Orchard Park, NY 14127

Cincinnati Bengals
200 Riverfront Stadium
Cincinnati, OH 45202

Cleveland Browns
80 First Ave.
Berea, OH 44017

Denver Broncos
13655 Broncos Parkway
Englewood, CO 80112

Houston Oilers
6910 Fannin St.
Houston, TX 77030

Indianapolis Colts
P.O. Box 535000
Indianaplis, IN 46253

Jacksonville Jaguars
One Stadium Place
Jacksonville, FL 32202

Kansas City Chiefs
One Arrowhead Dr.
Kansas City, MO 64129

Miami Dolphins
Joe Robbie Stadium
2269 NW 199th Street
Miami, FL 33056

New England Patriots
Foxboro Stadium
Route 1
Foxboro, MA 02035

New York Jets
1000 Fulton Ave.
Hempstead, NY 11550

Oakland Raiders
332 Center St.
El Segundo, CA 90245
(offices are still located in LosAngeles at press time)

Pittsburgh Steelers
300 Stadium Circle
Pittsburgh, PA 15212

San Diego Chargers
P.O. Box 609609
San Diego, CA 92160

Seattle Seahawks
11220 NE 53rd St.
Kirkland, WA 98033

NATIONAL CONFERENCE FOOTBALL TEAMS

Arizona Cardinals
P.O. Box 888
Phoenix, AZ 85001

Atlanta Falcons
2745 Burnett Road
Suwanee, GA 30174

Chicago Bears
Halas Hall
250 N. Washington
Lake Forest, IL 60045

Carolina Panthers
227 West Trade St.
Suite 1600
Charlotte, NC 28202

Dallas Cowboys
Cowboys Center
One Cowboys Pkwy.
Irving, TX 7506

Detroit Lions
Pontiac Silverdome
1200 Featherstone Road
Pontiac, MI 48342

Green Bay Packers
1265 Lombardi Ave.
Green Bay, WI 54307

Minnesota Vikings
9520 Viking Dr.
Eden Prairie, MN 55344

New Orleans Saints
6928 Saints Dr.
Metairie, LA 70003

New York Giants
Giants Stadium
East Rutherford, NJ 07073

Philadelphia Eagles
Veterans Stadium
Broad St. & Pattison Ave.
Philadelphia, PA 19148

San Francisco 49ers
4949 Centennial Blvd.
Santa Clara, CA 95054

St. Louis Rams
100 N. Broadway, Ste. 2100
St. Louis, MO 63102

Tampa Bay Buccaneers
1 Buccaneer Place
Tampa, FL 33607

Washington Redskins
21300 Redskin Park Dr.
Ashburn, WA 22011

NATIONAL HOCKEY LEAGUE

Anaheim Mighty Ducks
The Pond
P.O. Box 61077
Anaheim, CA 92803

Boston Bruins
Boston Garden
150 Causeway St.
Boston, MA 02114

Buffalo Sabres
Memorial Auditorium
140 Main St.
Buffalo, NY 14202

Calgary Flames
Olympic Saddledome
P.O. Box 1540, Station M
Calgary, Alberta,
Canada T2P 3B9
(Note: first-class mail to Canada requires extra stamps)

Chicago Blackhawks
1901 West Madison St.
Chicago, IL 60612

Dallas Stars
901 Main St.
Suite 2301
Dallas, TX 75202

Detroit Red Wings
Joe Louis Arena
600 Civic Center Dr.
Detroit, MI 48226

Edmonton Oilers
Northlands Coliseum
74241 118th Ave.
Edmonton, Alberta,
Canada T5B 4M9
(Note: first-class mail to Canada requires extra stamps)

Florida Panthers
100 North East Third Ave.
10th Floor
Ft. Lauderdale, FL 33301

Hartford Whalers
242 Trumbull St., 8th Fl.
Hartford, CT 06103

Los Angeles Kings
Great Western Forum
3900 W. Manchester Blvd.
Inglewood, CA 90306

Montreal Canadiens
Montreal Forum
2313 St. Catherine St. West
Montreal, Quebec,
Canada, H3H 1N2
(Note: first-class mail to
Canada requires extra stamps)

New Jersey Devils
Meadowlands Arena
P.O. Box 504
East Rutherford, NJ 07073

New York Islanders
Nassau Veteran's Memorial
Coliseum
Uniondale, NY 11553

New York Rangers
4 Penn Plaza, 4th Fl.
New York, NY 10001

Ottawa Senators
301 Moodie Dr.
Suite 200
Nepean, Ontario,
Canada K2H 9C4
(Note: first-class mail to
Canada requires extra stamps)

Philadelphia Flyers
The Spectrum
Pattison Place
Philadelphia, PA 19148

Pittsburgh Penguins
Civic Arena
Pittsburgh, PA 15219

Quebec Nordiques
Colisee de Quebec
2205 Avenue du Colisee
Quebec City, Quebec,
Canada G1L 4W7
(Note: first-class mail to
Canada requires extra stamps)

St. Louis Blues
St. Louis Arena
5700 Oakland Ave.
St. Louis, MO 63110

San Jose Sharks
525 West Santa Clara St.
San Jose, CA 95113

Tampa Bay Lightning
501 East Kennedy Blvd.
Suite 175
Tampa, FL 33602

Toronto Maple Leafs
Maple Leafs Garden
60 Carlton St.
Toronto, Ontario,
Canada M5B 1L1
(Note: first-class mail to
Canada requires extra stamps)

Vancouver Canucks
Pacific Coliseum
100 North Renfrew St.
Vancouver,
British Columbia,
Canada V5K 3N7
(Note: first-class mail to
Canada requires extra stamps)

Washington Capitals
USAir Arena
Landover, MD 20785

Winnipeg Jets
Winnipeg Arena
15-1430 Maroons Road
Winnipeg, Manitoba,
Canada R3G 0L5
(Note: first-class mail to
Canada requires extra stamps)

Ears to You
Earrings

A lady can never have too many earrings. Accessories are really necessities! With this offer you will get **2 pairs of fashion earrings** from a variety of colors, styles, and shapes. Just specify your preference for post, hoop, or dangle drop styles. Some of this quality designer jewelry originally retailed for as much as $10 a pair!

> **Send:** $2.00 P&H
>
> **Ask For:** 2 Pairs of Fashion Earrings
>
> **Mail To:** Surprises & Jewelry
> P.O. Box 1052
> Orange, CT 06477

Snap To It
Cat Treats

P leasing your cat is a snap with a **sample box of Cat Snaps.** Your favorite kitty won't be able to resist these flavor-filled tablet treats. Cat Snaps help to keep your cat or kitten in good health with a glossy coat, and they contain natural vitamins and minerals not normally found in daily cat food. This 90-tablet supply is enough for 2 to 6 weeks.

> **Send:** $2.00 P&H
>
> **Ask For:** Sample Box of Cat Snaps Treats
>
> **Mail To:** Prime Pet Products
> P.O. Box 2473
> Beverly Hills, CA 90213
>
> **Limit:** 1 per address

Stick to Studying
· ·
Academic Reward Stickers

Your students will feel like winners when you give them these **200 colorful awards 'n' trophies mini stickers.** These 1/2" round stickers come in an assortment of bright designs you can use to praise student effort and achievement. Send for them today to take the studying blues away!

Send:	$1.00 P&H
Ask For:	Awards 'n' Trophies Mini Stickers
Mail To:	The Very Best P.O. Box 2838, Dept. TR Long Beach, CA 90801

Straight A's
· · · · · · · · · · · · · · · · · · · ·
Education Tips

The producers of the "Math Made Easy" and "Reading Is Easy" video tutorials would like to show you the way to get your students to earn A's on their report cards. To give you a sampling of what their acclaimed videotapes can do for kids' grades, they will send you a **FREE brochure, "20 Math & Reading Tips to Pave the Way to an A."**

Phone Toll-Free:	1-800-MY20TIPS
Ask For:	"20 Math & Reading Tips to Pave the Way to an A"

A Dilly of A Lesson Plan

Agricultural Information

Where does food come from? *A Marketing Dill-Emma* is a **FREE comprehensive lesson plan** designed to teach students where food comes from by following the progress of a pickle from cucumber patch to grocery store shelf. This fun kit is designed for the third and fourth grades; however, it can be adapted for use at any elementary grade level. The kit includes activity sheets, a guide for individual student and interactive classroom projects, a full-color poster, and plenty of background for teachers. The unit also comes with a packet of cucumber seeds to grow in the classroom.

Send: Your request on school letterhead

Ask For: Pickle Lesson Plan

Mail To: Pickle Lesson Plan Dept. FR-T
P.O. Box 767
Holmdel, NJ 07733

A Few Lines to Save You Money

Money-Saving Tips

Savvy Discounts is offering a **FREE** eight-page **sample issue** of the *Savvy Discounts Newsletter,* which is full of easy and useful money-saving tips that promises to save you at least $840 each year you subscribe. This remarkable quarterly shows you how to spend less on almost everything you buy: from little-known secrets that lower your phone bill to getting a bargain on a new car, from luxury vacations at half price to the best deals in mail order.

Send: Your name & address

Ask For: Sample copy of *Savvy Discounts*

Mail To: Savvy Discounts Newsletter
P.O. Box 96
Smyrna, NC 28579

Animal Issues
Animal Rights Newsletter

You and your students can become educated and involved in helping endangered species by sending for a **FREE issue of** *KIND (Kids in Nature's Defense) News,* a student newspaper all about kindness and compassion for people, animals, and the Earth. You can also receive a **FREE "Student Action Guide,"** which provides step-by-step instructions for forming an earth/animal protection club, holding meetings, and planning activities.

Send:	Your name & address
Ask For:	Sample Issue of *KIND News* and FREE "Student Action Guide"; specify edition for grades K–6 or 7–12
Mail To:	NAHEE, Dept. FF P.O. Box 362 East Haddam, CT 06423
Limit:	1 per address

Learn to Have Fun
Learning Guide

Today's electronic toys cleverly combine learning with entertainment. But how do teachers and parents who grew up using flashcards and Lincoln Logs sort through the high-tech jungle to find the best educational toys for their kids? Request a **FREE copy of "Smart Play: A Guide to Learning & Discovery with Toys."** It explains how to shop for the best educational tools and activities.

Send:	A long SASE
Ask For:	"Smart Play Guide"
Mail To:	VTECH Smart Play 380 W. Palatine Rd. Wheeling, IL 60090

Study This Catalog!
••••••••••••••••••••••
Educators Catalog

A vailable to teachers and parents, this **FREE catalog** of low-cost publications and videos offered by the **California Department of Education** is a must-have. There are nearly 400 publications included in the catalog on a wide range of subjects that are sure to benefit both you and your students.

Send:	Your name & address
Ask For:	Catalog of Publications and Videos
Mail To:	CA Dept. of Education Publication Sales
	P.O. Box 271
	Sacramento, CA 95812-0271

Useful Tips
••••••••••••••••••••••
Easy-to-Use Glue

B lobs and blobs. Plops and puddles. When you want just a dribble, you get a torrent. That's the trouble with ordinary glue bottles and adhesive dispensers—but not with the fabulous **Craftip syringe dispensing kit**. This kit includes two reusable, dishwasher-safe, 7" syringes with 3" translucent barrels that hold 1/2 oz. Each dispenses glues, paints, oils, and almost any liquid with controlled precision. One syringe has a needle tip designed for thinner liquids; the other has a tapered tip for thicker, heavier products.

Send:	$1.85 P&H
Ask For:	Syringe Dispensing Kit
Mail To:	Bright Packaging Products Inc.
	P.O. Box 80
	Oceanport, NJ 07757

Patriotic Papers
Parchments

Instill in your young students a sense of the pride for our country's founders by introducing these **Colonial History Parchments** to your class. Select from either a reproduction of General George Washington's Call to Arms, or a pictorial history of the American Flag, from the Bunker Hill banner of the Revolutionary War to the 50-star flag of the present day. Each comes on parchment paper with an authentically aged look.

> **Send:** $2.00 P&H for 1; $3.25 for 2
> **Ask For:** Parchment; specify Call and/or Flags
> **Mail To:** S&H Trading Co.
> 1187 Coast Village Rd. #208
> Montecito, CA 93108

Copy of History
Poster

Did you know that of the many people who signed the Declaration of Independence, two became Presidents of the United States and two became Vice-Presidents? Unusual and interesting facts like this appear on the **parchment poster on the "Signing of the Declaration of Independence."** This 14" x 16" document presents a detailed history of the signing along with reproductions of the signatures that appeared on the original. The parchment is antiqued to look and feel authentically aged.

> **Send:** $2.00 P&H for 1; $3.25 for 2
> **Ask For:** Declaration
> **Mail To:** S&H Trading Co.
> 1187 Coast Village Rd. #208
> Montecito, CA 93108

Changin' Times
Health Brochure

Puberty is an often confusing and embarrassing time of life for kids. In an effort to bridge the gap during this challenging time of change, the Dial Plus Health & Beauty Awareness Council is offering a **FREE brochure entitled "Coming of Age: What You Really Need to Know."** This educational guide helps kids understand about body changes and rapid rates of maturation that occur at puberty.

Phone
Toll-Free: 1-800-258-DIAL

Stamp Out Fun
Teacher Stamps

Grading papers can be a tough task for teachers, but it can be fun with a **teacher's stamp.** You'll receive one rubber stamp mounted on a 1" wooden block selected from nine designs with an educational theme, such as a reward ribbon, a school bus, or an "apple from teacher." Also included are **10 mini stickers** that have a stamped design, creative ideas for stamping, a catalog, and a money-saving coupon for $1 off your next order.

Send: $1.75 P&H for 1; $1.25 for each additional stamp

Ask For: Teacher Stamp and Stickers

Mail To: Something for Everyone
P.O. Box 711
Woodland Hills, CA 91365

Communist Cash
Bank Notes

Whether you're teaching history, geography, or current events, this collection of authentic **Communist empire bank notes** will make a great teaching aid. You'll receive a collection of eight rubles and other notes from throughout the former Soviet Union. Some are emblazoned with crests, others have detailed drawings, and all of them make great collector's items.

> **Send:** $2.00 P&H
> **Ask For:** Communist Empire Bank Notes
> **Mail To:** Jolie
> Box 1375
> Roslyn Heights, NY 11577

Bayou for You
Food and Recipes

Straight to you from Chef Paul Prudhomme's K-Paul's Louisiana Kitchen are some great new seasonings that are both delicious and healthy for you! Send for **3 sample packets of Chef Paul Prudhomme's Poultry Magic, Vegetable Magic, and Hot & Sweet Pizza & Pasta Magic seasoning blends.** You'll also receive a catalog packed with dozens of fabulous Cajun food items, eight Chef Paul recipes, and a $5 coupon toward any purchase over $25.

> **Send:** $1.00 P&H
> **Ask For:** 3 Packets of Magic Seasonings
> **Mail To:** Magic Seasoning Blends
> P.O. Box 23342, Dept. MS
> New Orleans, LA 70183
> **Limit:** 1 per address

Pamper Your Feet
· ·
Shoe Insoles

Women, pamper your feet all day with **Feet Pleasers™** insoles. These amazingly thin soles provide protection from foot shock impact and give all-day comfort. The 3/4 length design won't cramp or crowd your toes and is perfect for those favorite flats or heels. These insoles regularly sell for $4.95, but now you can try a pair of Feet Pleasers for just a small shipping and handling fee. Constructed from Enduron™ foam material, Feet Pleasers absorb "step shock impact" to prevent tired, aching feet and legs.

Send: $2.00 P&H

Ask For: Sample pair of Feet Pleasers; specify shoe size

Mail To: Footsmart Products
507-B Maple Leaf Dr. Dept. 18
Nashville, TN 37210

Snack Attack
· ·
Snack Brochure

Don't let a snack attack ruin your diet. Learn to snack smart with the **FREE "Snack Savvy" brochure**, full of tips for healthful between-class and between-meal nibbling. Presented by The Quaker Oats Company, it includes four delicious recipes that are designed to curb your munchie madness with sensible nutrition.

Send: Your name & address

Ask For: "Snack Savvy" Brochure

Mail To: Snack Savvy, Dept. F
332 S Michigan Ave. Ste. 900
Chicago, IL 60604

Bite-Sized Delight
Health Food

For a delightful change of pace from processed sugar and chocolate candies, try **Aplets & Cotlets** (a 1.75 ounce **sample pack**) direct from Washington State. Made with pure apple and apricot purees, crunchy walnuts, natural flavors, and no preservatives, these confections are slow-cooked using a country family recipe. You'll also receive a money-saving coupon.

Send: $1.00 P&H

Ask For: Sample of Aplets & Cotlets

Mail To: Aplets & Cotlets
P.O. Box 202, Dept. XA
Cashmere, WA 98815

Pretty As a Picture
Postcards

Here's a great class project for a great price. Have your students bring in photos of their families or favorite trips and make up **Personalized Picture Postcards**. Order a pack of 6 or a pack of 100 and have your students simply affix the photos to the card's adhesive backings. Each card also has a pop-out easel for desktop display, and there's plenty of space on the back to write messages and addresses. Cards are available in 3 1/2" x 5" or 4" x 6" size.

Send: $1.55 P&H for 6; $8.00 for a pack of 100 (sent Priority Mail)

Ask For: Personalized Picture Postcard Pack; specify quantity and 3 1/2" x 5" or 4" x 6"

Mail To: Personalized Picture Postcard
P.O. Box 131
Buffalo, NY 14223

Caring About Child Care

Child Care Information

A child in day care spends a great deal of time outside the home. Your **FREE** copy of the **Ultimate Child Care Resource Catalog** is your source for books and information brochures on day care, parent/provider communication, and the best toys. It's an excellent resource for teachers, child care providers, and parents. You will also receive a **FREE** sample issue of the *Parent Care* **newsletter**, which is full of advice on nutrition, safety, and encouraging creativity in children.

Send: Your name & address

Ask For: Free Child Care Resource Catalog and Sample *Parent Care* Newsletter

Mail To: CanDan Publishing Co.
224B Radley Place SE
Calgary, AB Canada V0B 1BO
(Note: first-class mail to Canada requires extra stamps)

Quilting Quiz

Quilting Patterns

W hat's the first step in successful quilting? With this offer you will receive one 16-inch **quilt block pattern** printed on a single sheet of paper. Included are the necessary shapes and helpful instructions. The pattern pieces are full size, so there's no need for enlargement. You will receive a random selection from many popular designs.

Send: A long SASE

Ask For: Quilt Block Pattern

Mail To: Sturrock's Mercantile
Hwy. 90-A East
RR 5 Box 704
Hallettsville, TX 77964

You'll Fall for This

Fall Pin

Are the colder days of fall getting you down? Don't despair! Get a vibrantly colored **autumn leaf pin**, which is sure to brighten your day. The red, orange, and yellow pin can also be used as a tie tack. These pins are colored glass fused to metal, hand crafted, and kiln fired.

Send: $2.00 P&H

Ask For: Autumn leaf pin

Mail To: Gee Vee Enamels
P.O. Box 786
Pine Grove, CA 95665

Here's to Your Health

Health Advice

It's important to have certain health and safety information available at your fingertips. **The Will Rogers Institute**, a major research health facility and the country's largest distributor of health and safety information, is offering **FREE comprehensive booklets** on a variety of topics.

Send: Your name & address

Ask For: The following booklets by their titles

- *What Everyone Should Know About Drinking and Driving*
- *Shots for Tots*
- *Buckle Up Your Kids for Safety*
- *Alcoholic in the Family*
- *What Everyone Should Know About Child Abuse*
- *About Protecting Yourself from AIDS*
- *What Everyone Should Know About Crack or Rock Cocaine*

Mail To: Will Rogers Institute
785 Mamaroneck Ave.
White Plains, NY 10605

Miracle Worker
Skin Cream

Your face may feel clean after you wash it, but the top layer may still have dead skin, which can clog pores, prevent moisturizers from penetrating, and make fine lines appear larger. Unlike scrubs or loofah sponges, which can cause microscopic tears in the skin, "The Beautiful Skin Kit" gently removes dead skin. You can receive a **FREE 1/2 oz. sample of skin cream**. Dermatologists have dubbed the cream "miracle in a jar."

Send: $1.00 P&H
Ask For: FREE Sample Skin Cream
Mail To: Advanced Complexion Care Center
c/o Judith Olivia
260 Golden Days Dr.
Casselberry, FL 32707

Workout Wallet
Water-Proof Wallet

Picture this: It's time for your first aerobics class and you want to take some money along; you don't want to leave the house unlocked so you need to take your key. But your new workout suit doesn't have pockets. What do you do? Send for the **workout wallet**, which wraps around your wrist. The lightweight wallet is made of waterproof vinyl, and the attached Velcro™ keeps it securely on your wrist. It's thin enough to be comfortable, but wide enough to fit money, keys, and so on.

Send: $1.75 P&H
Ask For: Workout Wallet
Mail To: Neetstuf, Dept. FR-97
P.O. Box 353
Rio Grande, NJ 08242

No Yolks!

● ● ● ● ● ● ● ● ● ● ● ● ● ● ● ● ● ● ●

Egg Yolk Separator

Substituting extra egg whites instead of the yolk when cooking is a great way to cut down on fat and cholesterol. With this offer you will receive a **plastic egg yolk separator**, which quickly and easily separates the egg white from the yolk. You can also get a **4-in-1 measuring spoon**, which has tablespoon, teaspoon, 1/2 teaspoon, and 1/4 teaspoon sizes all in one spoon.

Send: $1.00 for 1; $2.00.00 for both

Ask For: Egg Yolk Separator and/or 4-in-1 Measuring Spoon

Mail To: Pineapple Appeal
538 Maple Dr.
P.O. Box 197
Owatonna, MN 55060

Just the Dirt, Ma'am

● ● ● ● ● ● ● ● ● ● ● ● ● ● ● ● ● ● ●

Cosmetics

Most soaps strip away the dirt but also remove your skin's own protective oils. Lite-Cosmetics has created cleansers that leave the skin's natural moisture levels intact. With this offer you'll get **3 samples** of new, natural **products from Lite-Cosmetics.** You'll receive "Evening Magic," a rich **Night Cream** containing natural proteins and vitamins with aromatherapy; **Eye and Throat Creme**, made with natural carrot oil to reduce the appearance of fine lines; and a non-greasy **Hand and Body Lotion.**

Send: $2.00 P&H

Ask For: 3 Samples of Skin Care Products

Mail To: Lite-Cosmetics
2124 El Camino Real, #201
Oceanside, CA 92054

Sensible Incentives

Student-Reward Pack

Students love incentive prizes, but they usually cost a lot of money for just a few. With this offer you'll receive **20 colorful assorted incentive prizes** for just $2 postage and handling. The assortment varies, but frequent prizes include stickers, erasers, pencil tops, mini coloring books, and jigsaw puzzles.

Send: $2.00 P&H

Ask For: 20 Assorted Incentive Prizes

Mail To: Surprises All Sizes #115
12 W. Willow Grove Ave.
Philadelphia, PA 19118

Picture This

Picture Frames

Special pictures call for special framing. With this offer you can receive **4 FREE mini picture frames**, measuring 4" by 5", and 4 separate cardstock backings. The frames are cut from brightly colored cardboard. Use them as they are, or stencil and hand paint them. Ideal as matting in a larger frame, and just the right size for your favorite student's school picture, these frames will really make your pictures go to the head of the class!

Send: Your name & address

Ask For: 4 Mini Picture Frames

Mail To: Woolie Works
6201 E. Huffman Rd.
Anchorage, AK 99516

Be Your
Own Hero
• • • • • • • • • • • • • • • • • • •
Learning Pack

Students need to develop a positive self-image. You can help build a child's self-esteem through a free packet entitled **America's Heroes and You.** The heroes come from various periods in American history and include people like Thomas Jefferson, Eleanor Roosevelt, and Cesar Chavez. This packet was designed to help inspire children of elementary and junior high levels through quotes, descriptions of the heroes' lives, discussion questions, and suggested activities.

Send: $2.00 P&H

Ask For: America's Heroes and You Educational Packet

Mail To: America's Heroes Offer
P.O. Box 16167
San Diego, CA 92176

Don't Leave
Home Without It
• • • • • • • • • • • • • • • • • • •
Phone Information Card

With this **Safety Phone Card,** you'll never forget to leave important phone numbers for sitters or others when you go out. The card includes space for the numbers of doctors, neighbors, the hospital, poison control, and the police. It also comes with self-stick notes for those extra instructions and a plastic suction cup so you can stick it wherever you want. The back of the card even doubles as a Baby Sleeping Sign, to alert visitors to be extra quiet.

Send: $2.00 P&H

Ask For: Infant Safety Phone Card/Baby Sleeping Sign

Mail To: F & H Baby Products
157 Greenbriar Dr.
Chagrin Falls, OH 44022

Get Together
Food Tips

Every day is filled with memorable moments and tiny triumphs that give us a reason to celebrate with family and friends. Cracker Barrel Cheese would like to assist you with these special moments that call for entertaining or celebrating. Send away for their **FREE booklet "Get-Together Ideas from Cracker Barrel Cheese,"** and you won't be caught unprepared next time you have company.

Send: A long SASE

Ask For: "Get-Together Ideas from Cracker Barrel Cheese"

Mail To: Get-Together Ideas from Cracker Barrel Cheese
P.O. Box 490513
El Paso, TX 88549-0513

Game Time
Games Brochure

Milton Bradley—the maker of children's all-time favorite games Candy Land and Chutes & Ladders—has created a **FREE brochure called "Growing with Games: A Parent's Guide to Little Kids' Fun."** Specially designed to answer the questions of preschool teachers and parents, the easy-to-use guide is packed with valuable information, practical tips, and advice on how to select the right game.

Send: Your name & address

Ask For: "Growing with Games: A Parent's Guide to Little Kids' Fun"

Mail To: Growing with Games—FRBS
c/o Fleishman-Hillard
1330 Ave. of the Americas
New York, NY 10019

Pizzas, Tacos, Burgers, and More

Food Tips

"**Y**ou can eat delicious dishes in any restaurant and still lose weight," says Cheryl Sindell, nutritionist and author of ***Not Just a Salad: How to Eat Well and Stay Healthy When Dining Out.*** This guide offers hundreds of recommendations for ordering healthy when dining out. The foreword is written by world renowned Chef Wolfgang Puck. This 288-page book sells for $12.95 in stores, but you can have it delivered to you for only $4.50! Cheryl Sindell will also autograph copies by request.

Send: $4.50 P&H and a self-addressed label

Ask For: *Not Just a Salad* Book

Mail To: Cheryl Sindell, Nutritionist
P.O. Box 49-1955
Los Angeles, CA 90049

Staple It

Mini-Stapler

Teachers, if you are looking for an easy-to-use small stapler, here is the answer for you! Scribbles and Giggles is offering you their **colorful mini-stapler** for only $2. The stapler can be personalized with your name and comes complete with 400 staples. It is easy to use and more practical than those heavy metal staplers.

Send: $2.00 P&H along with your first name printed clearly and a phone number in case there are any questions.

Ask For: Personalized stapler

Mail To: Scribbles and Giggles
1402 Woodland Dr.
Santa Paula, CA 93060

Stars and Hearts Forever

Puff-Up Sponges

For quick and easy fun, send for these **4 puff-up sponge shapes.** Dip them in water and they expand to their full size. You'll receive two 3" sponges and two 1" sponges in the shape of hearts and stars. Just add a little paint to each sponge (not included) and have your students decorate their favorite bulletin boards, folders, or even create a personalized T-shirt to bring home to Mom or Dad.

Send: $2.00 P&H

Ask For: 4 Heart and Star Sponge Shapes

Mail To: Celebrations of America
P.O. Box 280 Dept. FB
Pottsville, AK 72858

Stick to Teaching

Stickers

After correcting just a few test papers, do they all start to look the same? Why not make them all different and give your students special recognition with this **assortment of 5 sticker sheets.** Each sheet contains approximately 12 iridescent stickers that might include award ribbons, school supplies, letters of the alphabet, butterflies, hearts, celestial figures, and clown faces.

Send: $2.00 P&H

Ask For: 5 Sheets of Teacher Stickers

Mail To: J. McDaniel
P.O. Box 13556
New Bern, NC 28561

Snow What?

Snowflake Earrings

It's never too early to start planning for the holiday season. Why not add a little festive spirit to your ensemble with a **pair of sterling-silver-plated snowflake earrings.** The 1" earrings dangle from silver hooks and are painted white to match any outfit. And remember: There's more happiness in giving than in receiving, so why not send a pair to a friend, or even to a special student.

Send: $1.00 P&H

Ask For: Snowflake earrings

Mail To: Chipmunk Valley Crafts
P.O. Box 47056
Indianapolis, IN 46247-0056

Collector's Guidelines

Collector's Guide

If you are an avid collector and want information about news, notes, and inside secrets for collecting, then a **FREE copy of *Collector's Guidelines*** may be just the publication for you. Along with various articles about numerous collections and hobbies, *Collector's Guidelines,* a monthly newsletter, contains sections with questions and answers, and advertisements that may help you find the collector's items you've been looking for.

Send: A long SASE

Ask For: Sample copy of *Collector's Guidelines* newsletter

Mail To: Collector's Guidelines
1390 Carling Dr., Ste. 108
St. Paul, MN 55108

Creative Jewelry
• •
Fashion Accessories

If you are looking for a way to enhance and brighten a child's or your own accessory collection, you need not look any further. For only $2 you can either have **3 pairs of children's or adult's earrings, or 12 assorted children's hair goods.** The earrings range from small teddy bears to elegant flowers. They are all made for pierced ears and come in different shapes and colors. The children's hair goods are an array of bright and colorful clips, rubber bands, and combs.

Send: $2.00 P&H for 1 selection;
$3.25 for both items

Ask For: 3 Pairs of Earrings (specify child or adult style) or Assorted Children's Hair Goods

Mail To: Surprises and Jewelry
P.O. Box 1052
Orange, CT 06477

Animal Sponges
• •
Puff-Up Sponges

Drop it in water and watch your **puff-up sponge** grow into a colorful ally in the war against grime! A panda, koala, elephant, tree frog, rhino, snow leopard, gorilla, or turtle could be your kitchen or classroom's newest best friend. You will be sent one randomly selected animal from the sponge zoo. You may even want to order more than one sponge to give to your students as gifts or rewards.

Send: $2.00 P&H

Ask For: Puff-Up Animal Sponges

Mail To: Neetstuf, Dept. FR-AN
P.O. Box 353
Rio Grande, NJ 08242

Good Nutrition

Food Tips

Teaching your kids and your students about proper eating habits can be extremely frustrating. You can tell them to eat vegetables, but they are more interested in candy bars. The makers of Flintstones vitamins have put together a **FREE booklet entitled "Broccoli or Brownies? Building Healthy Eating Behaviors in Your Child."** It will provide you with helpful information you need to make a strong case for good nutrition.

Send: Your name & address

Ask For: Broccoli or Brownies Brochure

Mail To: Broccoli or Brownies
c/o Flintstones Vitamins
303 E. Wacker Dr., Ste. 440
Chicago, IL 60601

Make Turquoise Your Choice

Earrings

Sherry Ward, a jewelry artist whose creations have been featured in numerous craft shows, is offering a **pair of sterling silver/turquoise dangle earrings.** Completely hand-crafted, these earrings are made from genuine turquoise and sterling silver beads and dangle about 1" from silver hooks. The artist backs up her work with a 100% money-back guarantee if you are not completely satisfied and offers a free, "no questions asked" repair of damaged merchandise that is returned.

Send: $2.00 P&H

Ask For: 1 pair of sterling silver/turquoise earrings

Mail To: S. Ward
P.O. Box 3208
Oxford, AL 36203

A Matter of Consent
....
Medical Safety Form

Before you embark on a class field trip or even allow students to run around in the schoolyard, it's very important to take precautions for their safety. One important item to have on file is this **FREE Medical Treatment Form**, to be signed by parents or guardians, which lists important information about family physicians and insurance policy numbers.

Send:	A long SASE
Ask For:	Medical Treatment Form
Mail To:	Practical Parenting
	Dept. 1/FB-JR
	Deephaven, MN 55391
Limit:	1 per address

Lite Reading
....
Recipe Bookmark

If you want to eat healthy, learn how to cook healthy. Lesson one starts with a **FREE recipe bookmark.** Each bookmark features a low-fat, low-sugar, low-salt recipe from Kathy Kochan's *De-lite-ful Appetizers* book. You'll also receive information on her other book, *De-lite-ful Desserts*.

Send:	A long SASE
Ask For:	De-lite-ful Bookmark
Mail To:	De-lite-ful Books
	15 E. Main St.
	Mendham, NJ 07945

Telephone Directory
. . . .
LifeScan Card

Diabetes is not a rare condition. It actually afflicts about 14 million Americans. You should have updated information in the event that one of your students is a diabetic. An easy way to get the information is to send for your **FREE Tele-Library card from LifeScan**, which provides prerecorded information 24 hours a day on a variety of diabetes topics.

Send: A long SASE

Ask For: LifeScan Tele-Library Card

Mail To: LifeScan Tele-Library Card
485 Madison Ave., 4th Fl.
New York, NY 10022

Boiling Over
. . . .
Burn Prevention Information

If you can prevent young student chefs from scalding themselves, not only will you save them from unnecessary pain, but you'll also save them and their parents from the high cost of medical care. For informative prevention tips, send for a **FREE copy of *Be Smart: Stop Scalds.*** This simple flyer is packed with important details on preventing scalding accidents in the bathroom and in the kitchen.

Send: Your name & address

Ask For: *Be Smart: Stop Scalds* flyer

Mail To: National Institute for Burn Medicine
909 E. Ann St.
Ann Arbor, MI 48104

Lethal Lesson
Fire Safety Brochure

Fire prevention lessons involve more than just admonishing students not to play with matches. *Teaching Fire Safety to Kids* is a **FREE brochure** that tells you how to counsel and educate children who play with fire. If you don't think this is a big problem, consider the fact that 45% of school-age children are reported to have played with matches at least once, and 21% have actually set fires.

Send: Your name & address

Ask For: *Teaching Fire Safety to Kids* Brochure

Mail To: National Institute for Burn Medicine
909 E. Ann St.
Ann Arbor, MI 48104

World on A Wall
World Map

This full-color poster won't just brighten your classroom, it will brighten your students by teaching them valuable geographical facts. It's a 21" x 32" **world map poster** from George F. Cram Company, makers of some of the world's finest maps since 1867. Each map has been updated to show all the changes throughout Eastern Europe and the former USSR.

Send: $1.49 P&H

Ask For: World Map Poster CD-8-PST

Mail To: George F. Cram Co.
P.O. Box 426
Indianapolis, IN 46206

Right On Track
. . . .
Model Railroad Guide

Many teachers and parents remember playing with model trains, a hobby they can certainly share with kids. *Model Railroader* magazine has put together **Your Introduction to Model Railroading,** a **FREE** full-color guide to this fascinating hobby. Learn how to get started, design a layout, and actually build model railroads. This guide can lead to hours of classroom or family fun.

> **Send:** Your name & address
>
> **Ask For:** *Your Introduction to Model Railroading*
>
> **Mail To:** Marketing Dept.
> Kalmbach Publishing Co.
> 21027 Crossroads Circle
> Waukesha, WI 53187

Recreational Reading
. . . .
Children's Magazine

Every teacher eventually wants his or her students to tackle the works of Mark Twain and Charles Dickens. But a good way to get them interested in reading is to introduce them to a **sample copy of *Children's Playmate* magazine.** This educational publication includes short stories, puzzles, poetry, coloring pages, dot to dots, comics, an art page designed by *Children's Playmate* readers across the country, and much more.

> **Send:** $1.50 P&H
>
> **Ask For:** *Children's Playmate*
>
> **Mail To:** Children's Better Health Institute
> 1100 Waterway Blvd.
> Indianapolis, IN 46202

Get Out of The Dark

Health Advice

Teachers often see a side of children that sometimes parents miss. You may notice if a child is angry, irritable, or continually out of sorts, and this **FREE** publication will assist you in answering many questions centering on the causes of these behavior patterns. **"Is Your Child Depressed?"** is helpful reading material for every school teacher and parent.

Send: A long SASE

Ask For: "Is Your Child Depressed?"

Mail To: Dr. Joel Herskowitz
30 Arch St.
Framingham, MA 01701

Heart Like A Wheel

Tire Brochure

A FREE 15-page car care **informational brochure from Firestone Tires** has finally been published in easy-to-understand English. Every nonmechanic ought to appreciate this "mini course" in how to better understand his or her car's operation. Professional auto racer (and certified mechanic) Pat Lazzaro has put together plenty of helpful information in this publication. A handy car maintenance chart is even included. Best of all, this brochure is available FREE of charge by calling a toll-free telephone number.

Phone Toll-Free: 1-800-9-FIRESTONE

Ask For: Car Care Tips Brochure

Trial Offer

History Information

Whether you're teaching history, social studies, or current events, there will come a time when you need to discuss every American's right to trial by jury. "**The American Jury**" is a **FREE** publication that explains the privilege and importance of serving on a jury, describes jury selection procedures, the role jurors play in trials, and the difference between criminal and civil cases. At no cost to you, it's an open-and-shut case.

> **Send:** A long SASE
>
> **Ask For:** "The American Jury"
>
> **Mail To:** The American Jury
> P.O. Box 3744
> Dept. FRB
> Washington, D.C. 20007-0244

Tips On Toys

Safety Tips

Anyone who cares about children knows that toy safety is more than just child's play. "**Play It Safe!**" gives details on how many of the 100,000 accidents children have with toys each year are actually preventable. You'll find advice on how to determine the safety of a toy and which ones to avoid altogether. You may even want to share this **FREE** information with members of the PTA.

> **Send:** A long SASE
>
> **Ask For:** "Play It Safe!"
>
> **Mail To:** Play It Safe!
> P.O. Box 3744
> Dept. FRB
> Washington, D.C. 20007-0244

A Growing Solution
Environmental Kit

"Trees of Life" has been making the world a better place for years, protecting the environment and providing food for the hungry. This program has planted fruit trees in Brazil, Nepal, India, Guatemala, and other countries. With a **"Tree Adventure Kit" sample carton and seeds**, you and your students will receive a carton to which you add dirt and the tree seeds to start growing your own gift to give the Earth.

Send: $2.00 P&H for 1; $1.00 for each additional kit

Ask For: Tree Adventure Kit

Mail To: Trees for Life
Freebies Offer
1103 Jefferson
Wichita, KS 67203

Notable Art
Notecards

These **4 art print notecards and accompanying envelopes** will make your greetings an extra special delivery. Each card features a beautiful print created by a talented artist from Santa Barbara, California. Each of the four cards showcases colorful art on the front. The artist's name and a short biography appear on the back, and the inside is left blank for your personal notes.

Send: $1.50 P&H

Ask For: 4 Art Print Notecards

Mail To: Women's Economic Ventures
1387 Schoolhouse Rd.
Santa Barbara, CA 93108

Frame the Fun
• •
Bowling Advice

Bowling is a fun way for you and your students to spend your spare time. Your **FREE copy of BIF's Fundamentals of Bowling** can tell you about this popular pastime and show you how to throw a strike, convert a spare, and more. This 10-panel brochure employs a funny cartoon character named BIF to instruct young bowlers on technique, and kids will also get a fun **bookmark** and colorful **stickers** that feature BIF!

Send:	A long SASE
Ask For:	BIF's Fundamentals
Mail To:	BIF & Buzzy—Freebies
	5301 South 76th St.
	Greendale, WI 53129-1192

Yo-Yo Yahoo!
• • • • • • • • • • • • • • • • • • •
Yo-Yo Trick Sheet

Has life got you at the end of a string playing "loop the loop"? Are you thinking of "skinnin' the cat"? You can learn all the in's and out's of these popular yo-yo techniques in **Duncan® Yo-Yo's FREE trick sheet.** Presented in a fun and easy-to-read comic strip style, this 2-sided flyer explains the top 10 tournament tricks including "skin the cat." And it's from Duncan, the people who made the yo-yo famous. So order now!

Send:	A long SASE
Ask For:	Yo-Yo Trick Sheet
Mail To:	Duncan Toys
	P.O. Box 5
	Middlefield, OH 44062

Gifted Children
Education Information

Every day you probably notice little special qualities that each of your students possesses, but how often do you try to help them enhance these specialties? Students with special talents shouldn't get overlooked. The National Association for Gifted Children wants to help you detect a gifted child so that he or she can begin to enjoy the special programs available. They are offering you **FREE state resource sheets, book lists, and a chart outlining gifted characteristics.**

Send: A long SASE

Ask For: State Resource Sheets, Book List, Chart Outlining Gifted Characteristics

Mail To: National Association for Gifted Children
1155 15th St., NW, Ste. 1002
Washington, DC 20005

"O" Pin Season
Olympic Pin

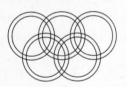

Atlanta 1996—the 24th Summer Olympics hosted by the U.S.A. To get the games started, Bill Nelson, the foremost collector in the country and a retired teacher, is offering you a **commemorative pin from the 1992 Barcelona Games.** The pin is exactly like the ones given to athletes and volunteers at the games, and it features the Barcelona logo. You'll also receive a **FREE issue of** *The Bill Nelson Newsletter,* a publication on pin collecting.

Send: $2.00 P&H

Ask For: Barcelona Olympics Pin

Mail To: Pins By Mail
P.O. Box 41630
Tucson, AZ 85717

Awesome Radio
BOOMERANG! Magazine

Inspire your students with stories, jokes, mysteries, and current events compiled by kids just like them. Request an **issue of *BOOMERANG!***—a magazine that comes on a cassette tape. This innovative 70-minute audiocassette turns short stories, world affairs, history, and other interesting topics into a media happening. The regular price is $7.95, but FREEBIES readers get a special discounted price of only $3, a savings of $4.95!

> **Send:** $3.00 P&H
> **Ask For:** *BOOMERANG!* issue
> **Mail To:** *BOOMERANG!* Magazine
> Box 261 F
> La Honda, CA 94020

Comic Book
Educational Comic

Most educators look down on comic books, but this book will change their minds! These wise publishers have created an educational comic book entitled ***Too Much, Too Little***, which presents the history of the U.S. monetary system and the establishment of the Federal Reserve System in lively comic book fashion. It's fun and educational! Order yours today.

> **Send:** Your name & address
> **Ask For:** Too Much, Too Little
> **Mail To:** Federal Reserve Bank of New York
> Public Information Materials
> 33 Liberty St.
> New York, NY 10045

A Hair Workout
Hair Care

Jingles International has come up with the solution to the limp, lifeless hair dilemma. **Hydro Kinetic Intensive Treatment** is a rich formula of herbal extracts, organic moisturizers, natural oils, and essential proteins that revitalize, strengthen, and revive your hair. It is excellent for permed or colored hair, contains no artificial colors, is not animal tested, and it can only be obtained through professional salons. You can receive a **1 oz. trial-size packet** good for two to four uses. Plus, you'll receive a buy-one-get-one-free coupon on a future purchase.

Send: $2.00 P&H

Ask For: Sample of Intensive Treatment

Mail To: Jingles International
115 Albany Post Rd.
Buchanan, NY 10511

100-Mile Dash
Health Packet

Respond to a physical challenge—join the **100-Mile Club,** which promotes exercise by asking members to take a pledge to complete 100 miles of exercise. It can be any kind of aerobic exercise, and 1 mile is credited for every 10 minutes of activity, such as walking, swimming, biking, and so on. If you're motivated to get fit and have fun doing it, send for this **FREE club membership.**

Send: A long SASE

Ask For: 100-Mile Club packet

Mail To: U.S. 100-Mile Club
P.O. Box 1208
Alturas, CA 96101-1208

A Great Combination
Classsroom Packet

In teaching, patience and understanding make a great combination. Here's another super combo. You'll receive a 9-piece combination of **3 full-sized eraser-tipped pencils, three 6-inch wooden rulers, and three 1 1/2-inch simulated calculator erasers** in several different cool colors. This combination is sure to rival P.E. and recess!

Send: $2.00 P&H

Ask For: Teachers' 9-Piece Combo

Mail To: Parker Flags & Pennants
5750 Plunkett St., Ste. 5
Hollywood, FL 33023

Animated Reading
Animated Bookmarks

Cartoons rule! And the kings of animation have got to be the Tiny Toons and the Animaniacs. Now your students can keep track of their favorite cartoon characters even when they're not near a TV set with these **2** randomly selected **Tiny Toons or Animaniac bookmarks.** They'll even help *you* keep your place in your favorite ACME do-it-yourself manual. The bookmarks are made of durable plastic and come in an assortment of colors, and each one features a wacky cartoon character.

Send: $1.50 P&H for 2

Ask For: Tiny Toons or Animaniac Bookmarks

Mail To: Anita Jones/FO
38-08 BCH CH Dr., #11B
Far Rockaway, NY 11691-1438

Body Talk
. . . .
Car Repair Brochure

As a car owner, your chances of needing the services of a collision repair and refinishing facility are greater than you think. It's important to know how to select a body shop and the right questions to ask once you've selected one. The National Institute for Automotive Service Excellence wants to help you make that tough decision with their **FREE brochure, "How to Choose the Right Body Shop."**

> **Send:** A long SASE
>
> **Ask For:** "How to Choose the Right Body Shop"
>
> **Mail To:** ASE Body Shop Brochure
> Dept. FR-B96
> P.O. Box 347
> Herndon, VA 22070

Asking for The World? Sure
. . . .
Mini Erasers

You'll feel like you've got the whole world in your hands—20 worlds, to be exact—with **mini Earth erasers.** Each colored eraser is 1-inch tall and makes for a strong and practical ecology teaching item. Your students are sure to work hard to get one of these. How much closer to owning the world can you get?

> **Send:** $2.00 P&H
>
> **Ask For:** Mini Earth Erasers
>
> **Mail To:** Parker Flags & Pennants, Inc.
> 5750 Plunkett St., Ste. 5
> Hollywood, FL 33023

Summer Break
• •
Car Repair Brochure

Get your car ready for summer's heat, dust, and stop-and-go traffic with the National Institute for Automotive Service Excellence's **FREE brochure, "Getting Your Vehicle Ready for Summer."** From your air-conditioning and cooling system to your brakes and tires, the brochure addresses many of the problem areas that can lead to mechanical failure and suggests easy ways to prevent them.

Send:	A long SASE
Ask For:	"Getting Your Vehicle Ready for Summer"
Mail To:	ASE Summer Brochure
	Dept. FR-S96
	P.O. Box 347
	Herndon, VA 22070

FREE FREE FREE

Something for nothing!!! Hundreds of dollars worth of items in each issue of **FREEBIES MAGAZINE**. Five times a year (for over 14 years), each issue features at least 100 FREE and low-postage-&-handling-only offers. Useful, informative, and fun items. Household information, catalogs, recipes, health/medical information, toys for kids, samples of everything from tea bags to jewelry—every offer of every issue is yours for FREE, or for a small postage and handling charge!

Have you purchased a "Free Things" book before—only to find that the items were unavailable? That won't happen with FREEBIES—all of our offers are authenticated (and verified for accuracy) with the suppliers!

❑ **YES** — Send me 5 issues for only $4.95
     (save $4.00 off the regular subscription rate!)
❑ **YES** — I want to save even more. Send me 10 issues
     for only $7.95 (save 70% off the cover price!)

❑ Payment Enclosed, or Charge my   ❑ VISA   ❑ MasterCard

Card Number _ _ _ _ _ _ _ _ _ _ _ _ _ _ _ _ Exp. Date _____

Name _____

Address _____

City _____ State _____ Zip _____

Daytime Phone#
(   ) _____
(in case we have a question about your subscription

Send to: FREEBIES MAGAZINE/Teacher Offer
1135 Eugenia Place, Carpinteria, CA 93013